TO SARAH PALIN, AND THE REST OF YOU WITH EVIL CRITIQUE

PROPHETESS SEALS

To Sarah Palin, and the Rest of You With Evil Critique
Written by Prophetess Tina Seals

This page left blank intentionally

To Sarah Palin, And the Rest of You with Evil Critique

Written by
Prophetess Tina Seals
Copyright 2015
All Rights Reserved.

To Sarah Palin, and the Rest of You With Evil Critique
Written by Prophetess Tina Seals

This page left blank intentionally

Dedication

This book is dedicated to all of you add holes in the United States Congress!

Blessings – get a clue, and get a real job, that you can actually do!

Prophetess Tina Seals

To Sarah Palin, and the Rest of You With Evil Critique
Written by Prophetess Tina Seals

This page left blank intentionally

Contents

Copyright Page

Tina Seals Books & Publishing

PO Box 53001, Houston, TX 77052

713-446-1683

http://www.tinaseals.com

tina@tinaseals.com

It's Amazing

It's amazing to me how you spend all of your waking moments attempting to analyze statements, about things, that you have asked me to write.

And then when your capacity, to understand, is limited, by your nature, as a heathen, and wicked person – you blame me.

Well you can't blame me that you are a low-life. And you can't blame me that you are a imperial racist.

You can't blame me that you are full of hate, and don't know how to do your job.

You can't blame me that I refuse to serve in Congress with you, because I don't like the looks of you, let alone, I can't stand your imperial attitudes.

You act like you own this country, or like someone died and made you king.

It's amazing to me, how you have so much time to criticize me, and yet you never do what you are to be doing.

If you spent half, just half of the time, you spend criticizing my "embarrassment to the GOP" or "Democratic Party" – when I never attempted to attach myself to either – you would probably be able to successfully:

1. Figure out how to help the people of this nation recover from this triple dip recession / depression you have led us into with your pork lust

2. Figure out that you all are the real embarrassment, and everyone outside of the country thinks you're a joke

3. Figure out how to actually create a bill that works

4. Figure out how to actually create jobs

5. Figure out how to write a working Universal Care bill – how about that smarty pants! When will you do that?

6. Figure out how to write an immigration bill

7. Figure out how to regulate commerce

8. Figure out how to recover all of the money lost in the Real Estate Market

9. Figure out how to stop using poor people's tax dollars to fund your pork bridges

10. Oh gee, how about this one. Figure out how to work together! Because you sure as hell haven't learned that yet!

It's amazing how you can find time, out of your busy schedule, to make video's about my lack of intelligence, and political ignorance. Yet you fail daily to see your own!

I never vowed to defend the constitution. So who is the real ass?

Who is the real failure here?

I guess that would be all of you, who spend your time, asking me, this non-degreed, ignorant, Negro, to tell you thinks, that you don't understand.

How about that stupid.

So who is the real dummy?

And Since You Didn't Understand Allow Me to Help You

1. You haven't done shit for the American people.
2. You are to f stupid to realize that when you create a bill, it must work with the economy – as it is – at the time of creation
3. The "stress testing thing" refers to the bills that you are creating and placing on an overburdened economy. Why the freak aren't you testing the vitality of the economy before you force your pork upon it? Because you're a f idiot.

4. Even an uneducated b like me knows that. And I am black, and don't own a bachelors. You dumb f.

Furthermore

You, and every generation of your family can kiss my Frito pie.

Peace and dread grease to you mf.

Some Take Away Points from Today's Book

1. Don't ask me shit and you won't have to worry about how ignorant it sounds
2. Don't ask my opinion if you don't want MY response.
3. If you don't understand what I am saying, ask me.
4. If you don't understand what I am saying, it's because you are lacking spiritual content. You are most likely heathen.

5. To attempt to classify me as a Republican, or Democrat, is to attempt to put me in the same closets you live in. I don't live in secret. I am who I am. And if you don't like that, you don't have to talk to me, ask me questions about the future, or read my "Intellectually Disable" Intellectual Property.

6. Did I ever ask for a seat in Congress? House or Senate?

7. Did I ever run for Assembly in any state?

8. Did I ever run for President?

9. Do I even have a Bachelor's degree, whereby you can measure, accurately, what I should know, and what I didn't learn, while in pursuit of my bachelor's degree?

10. Furthermore, I don't ask you questions, you ask questions of me. So, if you had all of the answers, why ask me questions?

11. And if my answers were so stupid, embarrassing, and "out there" – in "la la land"

– why do you make major decisions based on them?

12. Why do you read something into everything I say, as if you give prophetic weight to the things I say, if they are so asinine. Did I spell that right? Of course I didn't, I will let you spell it, since it begins most of your first names. Asses.

Furthermore

And yes, I used furthermore, as a subtitle, to my story, that most of you will suggest, lacks substance, because you are basing it on your "lack of creativity" in intellectual pursuits.

While we are throwing up such excellent critiques, allow me to throw up my own.

What the hell are you all slackers actually doing up there in congress, pilfering through minimum wage workers, hard earned tax dollars?

1. Oh excuse me, Sarah, and the rest of you assholes, have you created a viable jobs bill? NO.

2. Have you rehoused people in all of the foreclosed homes, your poor legislation, created? Uhm, no, you haven't.

3. Uh, did you actually finish coding Universal Care? Oh, no you didn't.

4. So while we are making fun, of my lack of education, and political astuteness, let's remember, I was denied my political heritage. I had a white dad, who was politically connected, yet got denied, because of you racist, the benefits of having a politically connected white dad.

But we all know my history, because parts of it are classified with the CIA, aren't they? Sure they are. And while you are picking fun at me, it really sounds like you kind of sickly admire me.

You seem to rely on me when you want to now things about the bible.

I Really Don't Care What You Think

Furthermore, I really don't give a flying flip what you think about me. Because if I see any of you "good ladies, and gents" on the street, and ask you for money for food, or even a meal, your "not-so-good-nature" will show up, and deny me of that!

So until you learn, how to be as great as I am, in real life, keep your ass in the congress, or wherever the flying flip you work, and do what you have been trying to do, for the last 2000 years – LEGISLATE SOMETHING SHALL YOU!

Oh and Please Excuse My Grammar / Ebonics

I am half Negro. You know, 1960 black ass, meets white meat, in the back of a car, and then you're born, kind of - 1960's.

If you don't understand what I am saying, have the courage to: 1.) visit your district in the hood, that you stole by failure to properly redistrict or gerrymander, 2.) buy an Ebonics dictionary, and actually learn how to communicate with the people you represent, or 3.) visit the hood and see just how ineffective you really are as an elected leader.

The End of Your Shenanigans

And so, if you didn't like the ending of the last book I wrote, wait until I vote, against your reelection.

Blessings –

Prophetess Tina Seals.

Sidebar:

The End. I'm voting your ass out! Please take that as a valid threat!

Now let's see if you can make sense of this. I am not voting for you anymore. I pray that you have the skills necessary to get a fast food job, like me!

Oh and Sarah, you are just the poster child for other failed elected leaders. I can't really vote you out, you quit. Spoof that NBC!

Fix Universal Care

This page left blank so you can take notes on your failed political career.

Analyze why you can't fix Universal Care - Congress!

Take notes:

_____

_____

_____

_____

_____

_____

_____

_____

_____

_____

Create a Living Wage

This page left blank so you can take notes on your failed political career.

Analyze why you can't create provide workers with a Living Wage - Congress!

Take notes:

_____

_____

_____

_____

_____

_____

_____

_____

_____

_____

Regulate Commerce

This page left blank so you can take notes on your failed political career.

Analyze why you can't Regulate Commerce - Congress!

Take notes:

_____

_____

_____

_____

_____

_____

_____

_____

_____

Restore the Economy

This page left blank so you can take notes on your failed political career.

Analyze why you can't restore the economy Congress!

Take notes:

_____

_____

_____

_____

_____

_____

_____

_____

_____

_____

Reform Social Programs

This page left blank so you can take notes on your failed political career.

Analyze why you can't reform SSI/SSD/Welfare Congress!

Take notes:

_____

_____

_____

_____

_____

_____

_____

_____

_____

_____

Create an Immigration Bill

This page left blank so you can take notes on your failed political career.

Analyze why you can't create an Immigration Congress!

Take notes:

_____

_____

_____

_____

_____

_____

_____

_____

_____

Team Work - Bipartisanship

This page left blank so you can take notes on your failed political career.

Analyze why you can't work with the president Congress!

Take notes:

_____

_____

_____

_____

_____

_____

_____

_____

_____

Create Jobs Congress

This page left blank so you can take notes on your failed political career.

Analyze why you can't create a Jobs Bill Congress!

Take notes:

_____

_____

_____

_____

_____

_____

_____

_____

_____

_____

_____

www.ingramcontent.com/pod-product-compliance
Lightning Source LLC
Chambersburg PA
CBHW061950280526
45787CB00004B/1804